READING POWER

Record-Breaking Animals

The Stick Insect
World's Longest Insect

Joy Paige

The Rosen Publishing Group's
PowerKids Press™
New York

Published in 2002 by The Rosen Publishing Group, Inc.
29 East 21st Street, New York, NY 10010

First Edition

Book Design: Michael DeLisio

Photo Credits: Cover, pp. 7a, 7b, 7c, 7d, 9, 13, 21 © Animals Animals; pp. 5, 11, 15, 17, 19 © National Geographic; p. 21a © Anthony Bannister; Gallo Images/Corbis; p. 21b, 21c, 21d © Indexstock

Paige, Joy.
The stick insect : world's longest insect / by Joy Paige.
   p. cm. — (Record-breaking animals)
Includes bibliographical references (p.   ).
ISBN 0-8239-5963-5 (lib. bdg.)
1. Stick insects—Juvenile literature. [1. Stick insects.] I. Title.
QL509.5 .P35 2001
595.7'29—dc21
                                    2001000872

Manufactured in the United States of America

Contents

Stick Insects

Stick insects live all over the world. They like warm temperatures best.

There are more than 2,500 different kinds of stick insects. They all have long bodies.

7

Most stick insects live on plants or in trees.

9

Hiding for Safety

Stick insects hide by looking like parts of a plant. They look like branches or twigs.

11

Stick insects can hang from branches. They can hang on a branch all day.

Stick insects do not move much during the day. Stick insects stay still so other animals will not know that they are there.

What Stick Insects Eat

Stick insects eat at night.
They eat the leaves on the
plants and the trees.

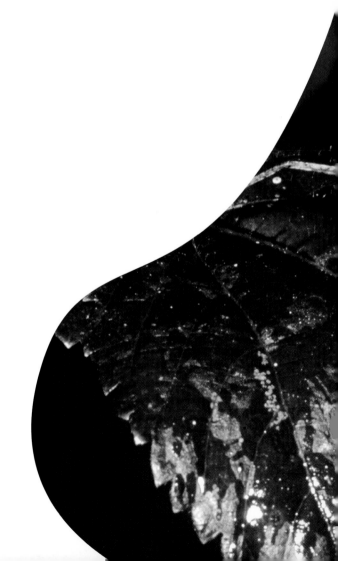

The Longest Insect

The longest stick insect ever seen was almost 22 inches long.

Stick insects are longer than any other insect. They are the longest insects in the world.

Cricket

Cockroach

Fly

Ladybug

21

Glossary

branch (**branch**) the part that grows from a trunk or stem of a plant

hang (**hang**) to be held from above

insect (**ihn**-sehkt) small animals with six legs and no bones

twigs (**twihgz**) small branches or shoots on a tree

Resources

Books
Walkingsticks
by Patrick Merrick
The Child's World, Inc. (1997)

Walking Sticks
by Adele D. Richardson
Smart Apple Media (2000)

Web Site
AES Bug Club Home Page
http://www.ex.ac.uk/bugclub/

Index

B
branches, 10, 12

L
leaves, 16

P
plant, 8, 10, 16

T
twigs, 10

Word Count: 131

Note to Librarians, Teachers, and Parents

If reading is a challenge, Reading Power is a solution! Reading Power is perfect for readers who want high-interest subject matter at an accessible reading level. These fact-filled, photo-illustrated books are designed for readers who want straightforward vocabulary, engaging topics, and a manageable reading experience. With clear picture/text correspondence, leveled Reading Power books put the reader in charge. Now readers have the power to get the information they want and the skills they need in a user-friendly format.